Rochester Castle
KENT

R ALLEN BROWN MA, DLitt, FSA

Professor of History, University of London, King's College

The great square keep of Rochester Castle has resisted destruction for over 800 years. Besieged more than once, it held out in 1215 for two months against King John. Battering the castle from huge stone-throwing engines, the King finally breached the keep by mining under it and setting fire to the pit props with the fat of forty pigs. Parts of the eleventh-century wall to the earlier castle remain, some built on the lower courses of the Roman city wall.

This handbook gives a history of Rochester Castle and those connected with it, followed, on page 19, by a description of the castle as it is today and how it was originally built. Plans and sections (pages 22–5) and many illustrations help to make the history and description more easily understood and a tour of the castle more interesting.

ENGLISH HERITAGE • LONDON

CONTENTS

3   HISTORY
3   Earliest castle
5   Gundulf 's castle
8   Building the keep and after
10 Siege of 1215
11 Repairs and improvements, 1220–60
14 Siege of 1264
17 Works of 1367–83
18 Later history

19 DESCRIPTION
19 Bailey
19 *Entrances and outer curtain wall*
26 *South and southeast curtain wall and Henry III's southeast tower*
27 *Edward III's east curtain wall and mural towers*
29 Keep
30 *Forebuilding, entrance vestibule and chapel*
32 *Basements of forebuilding*
33 *Plan and construction of main tower*
35 *Ground floor or basement*
35 *First floor*
35 *Second or principal floor*
38 *Third floor*
40 *Wallwalk and turrets*

42 GLOSSARY

PLANS
22 Site plan
24 Sections through keep
25 Floor plans of keep

© *Crown copyright 1969*
Previously published by HMSO 1980
Published by English Heritage, 1 Waterhouse Square, 138-142 Holborn, London EC1N 2ST
First published by English Heritage 1985
Second edition 1986, reprinted 1989, 1992, 1994, 1997, 2004, 2006, 2009
Printed in England by Park Communications
C30, 04/09   05826
ISBN 978 1 85074 106 0

Mixed Sources
Product group from well-managed forests and recycled wood or fiber
www.fsc.org Cert no. SGS-COC-2842
© 1996 Forest Stewardship Council
FSC

HISTORY

View from the southeast from an engraving by Samuel and Nathaniel Buck, 1735

Rochester has a distinguished history to which the castle has made its own distinguished contribution. The city (modern and medieval) was built within the walls of a Roman town, sited where the Roman Watling Street crosses the Medway on its route from London to Canterbury and Dover.

The first castle was raised here at the time of the Norman Conquest and is mentioned in Domesday Book (1086). This was rebuilt for William Rufus by Gundulf, Bishop of Rochester, between 1087 and 1089, to become one of the earliest castles in this country to be fortified in stone. To it there was added, in about 1127 in the reign of the next King, Henry I, the existing KEEP (the modern word, or DONJON, the contemporary word) in the form of a great rectangular tower, which is among the finest and oldest in all England [see the Glossary for an explanation of the terms printed in small capitals].

The existence of documentation to enable these earliest building phases of the castle to be positively dated is especially fortunate; the remainder of its architectural development in the medieval period is also very well recorded, as is its dramatic military history which witnessed three major sieges within two centuries of its foundation.

Earliest castle

Castles, the private fortified residences of princes and other lords, as opposed to the communal and national defences of Anglo-Saxon fortified cities and boroughs, were a Norman importation into England and a principal means whereby the Norman Conquest was achieved and the Norman settlement rendered permanent. It is not surprising, therefore, that the city of Rochester received a castle at a date very soon after 1066.

Domesday Book, containing the results of a survey of his new kingdom taken by William the Conqueror at the end of his reign, refers to land in Aylesford, Kent,

3

given to the Bishop of Rochester, in exchange for the land upon which the castle had been built. Gundulf's castle consisted of a walled enclosure literally following the lines of this original castle and, like its predecessor, surrounded on the three landward sides by a ditch or moat, of which the impressive remains can still be seen along the east side between the castle and the cathedral.

A long section of Gundulf's CURTAIN WALL remains along the west side towards the river, in part resting on the lower courses of the Roman city wall as a foundation, and heightened and strengthened in the thirteenth century (page 13). The southeast and eastern sections were rebuilt in the thirteenth and fourteenth centuries respectively (pages 13, 17), but a little more remains mutilated on the far side of Castle Hill to serve as the back-garden walls of several houses in the High Street.

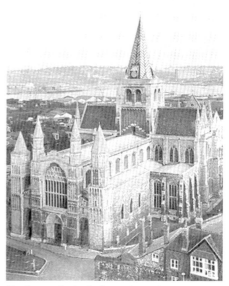

Rochester Cathedral seen from the keep

The main gateway from the city, later to be altered in the thirteenth or fourteenth century (page 17), stood more or less in the place of the present main entrance from Castle Hill. No evidence survives of mural towers on the curtain; the known earlier foundations of the southern of the two fourteenth-century towers on the east side of the castle (see the site plan on pages 22–3) are now thought to be those of a twelfth-century tower inserted into Gundulf's wall (page 27).

It appears that in the Conqueror's time both the city and the castle of Rochester were committed to his half-brother, Odo, Bishop of Bayeux. Before his disgrace and imprisonment in 1082 Odo was a dominant figure in Norman England and was entrusted with the earldom of Kent. The same Bishop Odo was to be the principal cause of the first siege of Rochester in 1088. In that year a large section of the Norman baronage (including Odo and his

brother Robert, Count of Mortain, with Geoffrey de Mowbray, Bishop of Coutances, and his nephew Robert de Mowbray, Earl of Northumberland, Roger de Montgomery, Earl of Shrewsbury, and Gilbert fitz Richard of Clare and Tonbridge), dismayed at the division of Normandy from England, which resulted from the Conqueror's disposal of his dominions at his death in 1087, supported the claims of the elder son Robert, then Duke of Normandy, against William Rufus, the younger son who had succeeded to the Kingdom of England.

Rochester was fortified by Bishop Odo against the King and became a rebel headquarters. The city was well placed both for raids upon London, or the devastation of Kent and, more particularly, the lands and lordships of Lanfranc, Archbishop of Canterbury, who had crowned Rufus and was Odo's enemy. According to the chroniclers Florence of Worcester and William of Malmesbury, who between

The castle as seen from the tower of the cathedral with the River Medway beyond. The site of the medieval bridge is at the extreme right of the picture

them give the most details of the ensuing campaigns, Rufus marched towards Rochester from London by way of Tonbridge where he captured the castle and wounded its lord, Gilbert fitz Richard.

Hearing that Odo himself had left Rochester for Pevensey, a castle of Robert, Count of Mortain, the King diverted his army there and took that castle with both his uncles in it. Bishop Odo was compelled to swear that he would yield Rochester, and to give effect to the promise Rufus sent him ahead with a small royalist force to call upon the garrison to surrender. Over-confident with Odo in their company, the royalists came to the city and called the townsmen to open the gates, 'for so the bishop in person and the absent King commanded.' The garrison, however, 'observing from the wall that the countenance of the bishop ill agreed with the words of the speakers' made a mounted sortie and captured the entire party, carrying both them and Bishop Odo in triumph into the town.

When the King heard of this he laid siege to Rochester, raising, we are told, a large force of native English for the purpose. According to Orderic Vitalis, this took place in May, and two siege castles were constructed to block any exit from the beleaguered fortress. The garrison, under their leaders, Bishop Odo, Eustace, Count of Boulogne, and Robert de Bellême, the son of Roger de Montgomery, Earl of Shrewsbury, plagued by heat, flies and disease, were compelled to seek terms which Rufus reluctantly granted. While the royal trumpets blew in triumph, they were allowed to march out with horses and arms, but were stripped of their lands in England.

Odo, Bishop of Bayeux, his English possessions lost a second time, returned to Normandy, whence he subsequently accompanied Duke Robert on the First Crusade and died on that expedition.

Gundulf's castle

The exact part played by the castle of Rochester in these events is not certain, for it is clear that the whole city was held by Odo against the King and was subsequently besieged, and it is generally to this that the chroniclers refer. Nor is it certain which castle, the first or second, was then in existence. In default of evidence to the contrary it seems likely that the construction of a new and more up-to-date castle would follow the campaign of 1088 with its emphasis upon the strategic importance of Rochester.

What is certain is that the second Rochester Castle was built for the King by Gundulf, Bishop of Rochester, between the accession of William Rufus in 1087 and the death of Archbishop Lanfranc in 1089. The *Textus Roffensis* (the early twelfth-century register of Rochester cathedral priory) preserves the memory of how it came about.

In the time of William the Conqueror, Archbishop Lanfranc had granted to the monks of Rochester the manor of Haddenham, in Buckinghamshire, which he himself had been given by the Conqueror but only for life. On the accession of William Rufus it was therefore necessary for both Lanfranc and Bishop Gundulf to seek a confirmation of the grant from the new King, who demanded the sum of £100 for the concession. Dismayed, the two prelates replied that they neither had so much money nor knew how to raise it.

At this stage Robert fitz Hamo and Henry, Earl of Warwick, mutual friends of both parties, King and bishops, suggested to the former that Gundulf, being skilled in masonry, might build a stone castle at Rochester instead of paying the money. At first Gundulf and Lanfranc were even more dismayed at this suggestion, fearing both the cost of the project and that the church of Rochester would afterwards be held responsible for its maintenance. Earl Henry, however, persuaded them that the castle could be built to the King's satisfaction for £40 at most, and that, once

built, it would be handed over to the custody of some layman, earl or sheriff, and not remain a charge upon Gundulf and his successors at Rochester. Thus the agreement was sealed, and Gundulf built the castle in stone at his own expense and at a cost in the event of £60, though, as it had been pointed out, this was no bad outlay in return for the perpetual possession by his church of a manor valued at £40 a year in Domesday Book.

Although the hypothesis was never archaeologically tested, modern accounts have followed E S Armitage in placing the earlier castle on the site known as the Boley Hill, south of the present castle and just outside the city [see site plan shown on pages 22–3, and E S Armitage, *Early Norman Castles of the British Isles*, London 1912, ppl95*ff*]. It was also thought to have been a MOTTE and BAILEY type of castle, i.e. one which consisted of a great mound of earth and a larger enclosure of the bailey, each defended by ditches, banks and PALISADES, and further strengthened by timber towers and other buildings. Excavations and re-examination of all the evidence have shown, however, that the first castle was in fact on the site of the present one rebuilt by Gundulf, the walls of which almost everywhere sit upon its earlier banks [see Colin Flight and A C Harrison, 'Rochester Castle, 1976,' *Archaeologia Cantiana*, xciv, 1978]. In consequence, the Boley Hill must be relegated either to an earthwork from which King John conducted his siege in 1215 (page 10), or to an outwork of the castle constructed after that siege – or perhaps to one of the two siege castles raised by Rufus, according to Orderic Vitalis, in the siege of 1088 (page 5).

Rochester Castle was thus from the beginning an enclosure of ditch and bank within an angle (here the southwest angle) of a pre-existing and former Roman fortified town, on the analogy of Pevensey or Portchester or, indeed, London. Nor on the same analogy do we have to postulate a motte, though, if there were one, it would have been in the vicinity of the present keep (page 8).

The new castle stood in the best part of the city, according to the *Textus Roffensis,* beside the river and guarding the approach to the medieval bridge across the Medway. Almost all of it survives except where the modern roadway called Castle Hill has been driven through its northeastern extremity (see the site plan on pages 22–3).

On the river or west side the perimeter followed the line of the Roman city wall, and made use of whatever remained of it, for a short stretch before parting company with it to run further south. On the three landward sides the castle was also defended by a strong ditch, and its banks or ramparts were of gravel to north and east, though in the southwest angle chalk rubble was piled against and over the remains of the Roman wall. From the emphasis placed by the *Textus Roffensis* upon the fact that the next castle, i.e. Gundulf's reconstruction, was of stone, it seems safe to conclude that the banks of the first castle were crowned by timber palisades. Some indication of the importance attached to the castle by the Normans of the first generation is given by the generous provision of feudal castle-guard service made for it, at least sixty FIEFS each owing the service of a knight being assigned to it.

Gundulf was a man of parts and a Norman bishop who has left his mark upon Rochester and also upon Kent and southeast England. Born about the year 1024 in the Vexin on the borders of Normandy, he became a clerk in the cathedral church of St Mary at Rouen. As a young man he made the pilgrimage to Jerusalem and subsequently became a monk at Bec, where Lanfranc was prior, where Anselm also became a monk at about the same time, and which was then becoming the most renowned of all the Norman monasteries.

When in 1063, before the conquest of England, Lanfranc was promoted to become abbot of Duke William's new foundation of St Stephen's at Caen he took the monk Gundulf with him, and Gundulf was again chosen to be one of his companions when, in 1070, Lanfranc was summoned to England to become the Conqueror's Archbishop of Canterbury. In 1077 Gundulf was appointed to the vacant SEE of Rochester, and became a model bishop as befitted the friend of Lanfranc and Anselm and a son of Bec. Amongst other good works, he rebuilt his cathedral church on the model of the archbishop's new Christ Church, Canterbury, installed monks there and began their CLAUSTRAL buildings, founded and built the nunnery at West Malling, Kent, with the enigmatic St Leonard's Tower nearby, and was instrumental in the building of many lesser churches in and about the Medway valley.

Most Norman archbishops and bishops in this age were great builders, but Gundulf was evidently more than a mere patron and employer of craftsmen. Robert fitz Hamo and Henry, Earl of Warwick, in suggesting to the King that Gundulf should build him a new castle at Rochester, stated that he was 'very competent and skilful at building in stone.' Nor was Rochester the only fortification with the building of which Gundulf was associated, for there is documentary evidence that he supervised the great work of the Conqueror's White Tower of London.

In all these undertakings it is probable that Gundulf's architectural role was that of a knowledgeable clerical administrator who knew how good work should be done and how to obtain it, and to his skill in this respect there is ample testimony, in the Tower of London, still guarding that city, and also in the considerable stretches of his wall at Rochester, still enclosing the castle site.

Keep and curtain wall from the east

Building the keep and after

In 1127 the next King, Henry I, issued a charter, the text of which survives. With the counsel of his barons, he granted the custody and constableship of Rochester Castle to Archbishop William de Corbeil and his successors at Canterbury in perpetuity. The knights who owed castle guard duty were to continue to serve in that respect, and the archbishops were further empowered to make 'a fortification or tower within the castle and keep and hold it forever.'

The grant is duly noted by the chronicler John of Worcester, and also by Gervase of Canterbury who adds that there 'the same archbishop [William de Corbeil] built a noble tower.' There is no doubt that this 'noble tower' is the present keep, which is thus positively dated and, having close affinities with the great tower at Castle Hedingham in Essex, helps to date that also.

The keep, in the form of a great tower, was in every sense the dominant feature of any castle that had one. It usually contained some of the finest residential accommodation, as is certainly the case at Rochester, Hedingham and the Tower of London, and served also as the military strongpoint and citadel, as the two subsequent sieges of Rochester were to demonstrate.

With its great tower standing four-square within the circuit of Gundulf's walls and the insertion of at least one mural tower in its curtain (page 27), the architectural development of the new castle of Rochester seems to have been complete for the remainder of the twelfth century, though it was carefully maintained, evidently at the King's expense at least during vacancies in the archbishopric. As well as many smaller sums at other times, over £100 were spent on the tower and castle by Henry II in 1172–73, according to the PIPE ROLLS, against the rebellion of his son, and the same source records an expenditure of £115 by King John in 1206 on the castle, its ditches, bridge, tower and other buildings.

The perpetual custody of Rochester Castle by the see of Canterbury also lasted throughout the twelfth century, and there is evidence of both Thomas Becket and Hubert Walter, as incoming archbishops, successfully asserting their rights in the matter. But a royal castle in the perpetual or hereditary custody of some other lord, whether ecclesiastical or lay, could seem nine parts private property, and it is likely that later kings came to regret the serious diminution of their control over so important a fortress, as certainly the potential danger of such an arrangement was to be dramatically shown in 1215.

While it seems clear that Hubert Walter as archbishop enjoyed the custody of Rochester under Richard I, it may be significant that letters patent of John placing the castle in Hubert's keeping are dated July 1202, three years after the King's accession. Without doubt later in his reign John came to an agreement with the next archbishop, Stephen Langton. (The King neither liked Langton nor wanted him at Canterbury, and to block his appointment he had defied the papacy for years, thereby involving his kingdom in an interdict and himself in a sentence of excommunication). Their agreement was that the castle should be in the hands of a royal constable, Reginald de Cornhill II, Sheriff of Kent, until Easter 1215, and subsequently until Easter 1216. Letters patent of the King, dated 25 May 1215, on the eve of Magna Carta, refer to this agreement and request, in the politest terms, that the castle should be transferred from Reginald de Cornhill to other royal custodians, who are to swear, as Reginald had done, to hand it back to the archbishop when the term is up, or sooner if peace should first be restored in the kingdom. The letter further requests that the castle may meanwhile remain under the archbishop's protection 'in such a way that by it no ill or harm shall come to us or our kingdom.'

According to the chronicler Roger of Wendover, soon after Magna Carta – which, dated 15 June 1215, was among other things a peace treaty between John and the rebels – Rochester was restored to Langton, but on 9 August letters patent were issued in the King's name which again refer to the original agreement and request the transfer of the castle to Peter des Roches, Bishop of Winchester and John's close supporter. What happened next is less than clear except that about the end of September a party of rebel barons entered Rochester to hold it against the King.

The chronicler Ralph of Coggeshall says that Langton refused to give up the castle at the King's request, but that the rebels, fearing he would be compelled to yield, seized it with the consent of its constable, named as Reginald de Cornhill. Reginald had formerly been the King's constable there, but must now presumably have been holding Rochester for the archbishop. He was certainly a latter-day opponent of John, since his lands were confiscated by the King on or before 2 October, and he was among those captured in the castle when it fell at the end of November.

The Barnwell annalist says also that Langton refused, 'I don't know why' to give up the castle to John as he had promised, and Wendover asserts that the archbishop handed over the castle to the King's enemies, 'with what conscience God only knows.' Stephen Langton left the country in mid September and the precise degree of his complicity and guilt perhaps remains uncertain. However, at this distance of time, and with insufficient and somewhat confusing evidence, it is not possible to rebut King John's unqualified charge of treason, expressed in a letter to Hubert de Burgh later in the year: 'For he [Langton] is a notorious and barefaced traitor to us, since he did not render up our castle or Rochester to us in our so great need.' It is in any case to be noted that after 1215 no further reference has been found to the perpetual custody of Rochester's royal castle by the Archbishops of Canterbury.

Siege of 1215

According to Roger of Wendover, the rebels seized Rochester in order to block King John's approach to London, which was their headquarters. The same author names William de Albini of Belvoir as commander of the rebel forces, and says that finding the castle bare of supplies they had little time to get in adequate provisions as John attacked on the third day. The strength of the occupying garrison is variously given by the chroniclers as 95–140 knights, with sergeants, crossbow-men and other ranks.

The King had spent the month of September 1215 mainly at Dover (with occasional visits to Canterbury), occupied, among other things, in recruiting stipendiary forces from the Continent as the political situation in England worsened. When he heard of the seizure of Rochester he lost no time in moving into the attack. He himself was at Rochester on Monday 13 October, having ridden from Dover along Watling Street via Canterbury, Ospringe and Gillingham. It seems likely, however, that the royalist forces were in action before his arrival, marching round south and west via Malling (where John is known to have been on 30 September, perhaps on reconnaissance, before returning to Canterbury and Dover). Ralph of Coggeshall says that the attack was launched from the river side of the city (*ex parte fluminis intercurrentis*), and both he and the knowledgeable Barnwell annalist record the first move as the capture and breaking of Rochester bridge to prevent any relief from London.

According to Coggeshall again, the first assault on the bridge was beaten off, but

on 11 October the King's forces entered the city by surprise and the siege of the castle began. What followed is the greatest operation of its kind in England up to that time, impressive by any standards, occupying the better part of two months before the castle finally fell on 30 November, conducted throughout in classic fashion by King John in person, who thereby showed, though neither for the first nor last time, a military ability which is often denied him. 'Our age,' wrote the Barnwell chronicler, 'has not known a siege so hard pressed nor so strongly resisted.' After it, he added, 'few cared to put their trust in castles.'

It is thought that King John may possibly have set up his command headquarters on the Boley Hill, and it is certain that great stone-throwing engines, the artillery of the age, were at once erected to pound the defences. There were five of them according to the Barnwell chronicler and Roger of Wendover writes of a ceaseless barrage by day and night both from them and from the small-arms of bows and crossbows, one contingent of the royalist forces relieving the other. According to the former source the engines battered a breach in the bailey walls, but Wendover states that the projectiles achieved little and John was forced to employ the device of undermining to gain entry. It seems that he is right, for a writ was sent, dated as early as 14 October, to the reeves of Canterbury commanding the urgent manufacture 'by day and night of as many picks as you are able,' to be sent with all speed to the King at Rochester. What may have been a mining trench of this period was found in recent excavations north of the northern of the two mural towers on the east side of the castle (*Archaeologia Cantiana*, xciv, 38).

Meanwhile, the baronial leaders at London had made an abortive attempt to relieve Rochester on the 26 October, advancing with 700 horse as far as Dartford where they turned back – Wendover says, sarcastically, because they met a gentle south wind, and the Barnwell chronicler says because they learnt that the King was coming against them and they had insufficient infantry to withstand him.

At Rochester, when Gundulf's wall had been breached and entry secured into the bailey, the defenders withdrew into the strong-point of the keep. Ancient and strong, we are told, it stood impervious to projectiles, and John had to set his miners to the dauntingly difficult task of breaching its massive construction. The mine was set beneath the southeast angle, presumably in near proximity to the breach in the bailey wall. An urgent writ, dated at Rochester on 25 November, commands Hubert de Burgh, the King's justiciar, to 'send to us with all speed by day and night forty of the fattest pigs of the sort least good for eating to bring fire beneath the tower.' In an age before gunpowder the pig fat was required to fire the pit props shoring up the undermined foundations. John's mine was successful, a whole section of the great tower came down, and to this day there is at Rochester a monument to those forty pigs in the cylindrical southeast angle of the keep, rebuilt in Poitevin fashion after the war was over (pages 30, 40).

Even this considerable achievement of siege-craft and military engineering did not, however, bring about the immediate capitulation of the castle, though the end was near. When one side of the keep was breached, the defenders withdrew behind the cross-wall (page 30) into the other, and continued their resistance – 'for such was the structure of the stronghold,' as the Barnwell chronicler observed, 'that a very strong wall separated the half that had fallen from the other.' By then, however, the near desperate state of the garrison was made worse by a growing shortage of provisions. They were reduced to a diet of horse flesh and water, 'which bore hardly on those who had been brought up in luxury' (Barnwell). First they expelled those of their number least capable of fighting – many of whom are said to have had their hands and feet amputated by the King's army – and soon afterwards all of them were captured.

According to Roger of Wendover, John wanted to hang all noble members of the garrison (which by law and custom of war as then waged he was probably entitled to do, as the castle had been taken by storm) but was dissuaded by one of his captains, Savaric de Mauléon, on the grounds that it would lead to retaliation against royalist garrisons in future and come to weaken their will to resist. The Barnwell chronicler says that in the event, in spite of the King's wrath, he hanged only one captured rebel from the castle, a crossbowman whom he had maintained since boyhood. But the Chancery enrolments and the chronicles alike contain long lists of noble and knightly prisoners, including William de Albini and Reginald de Cornhill, sent for incarceration to Corfe and other royal castles.

The siege completed, John divided his army into two parts, sending one into East Anglia, and himself proceeding with the other through Malling and Winchester up towards the north of his kingdom, to spend his Christmas at Nottingham. A little of the pomp and panoply of medieval warfare as waged by kings and princes is perhaps still reflected in a royal writ, dated at Malling on 8 December, ordering sufficient money to be paid to William Longsword, Earl of Salisbury and the King's brother, that he might leave the town of Rochester with due honour.

Repairs and improvements, 1220–60

In 1216, as the fortunes of war changed, Rochester Castle was evidently captured by Prince Louis of France, soon after his

Interior of the drum tower on the southeast corner of the curtain wall, built by Henry III

Keep and curtain wall from the southeast showing the rebuilt corner of the keep with its cylindrical turret. The powerful drum tower with its two tiers of arrow loops also dates from the repairs of Henry III

Southwest view of the keep and curtain wall

landing in this country as the new leader of the opposition to King John, invited by the rebel barons to take the crown of England. No details of this event exist and in the following year, 1217, when John was dead and Louis had returned to France, peace was restored in the kingdom.

Rochester came back into the hands of the government of the new young King, Henry III, John's son, then aged nine. The urgent need was the repair of the severely damaged fortress. In the next twenty years some £680 were spent upon the castle, most (£530) specifically upon the keep. In addition, in 1225–26 some £300 were spent upon the improvement of the defences of the city by digging a deep ditch outside its walls. To the south this took in the Boley Hill site, from which John may have conducted his siege, with the evident intention of denying that position to any future attacker.

At the castle some of the first work to be undertaken was the restoration and strengthening of the bailey wall, but though in 1221 there is reference to its repair, with the repair of certain buildings within the castle and the construction of a new chapel and chamber, it is not until December 1223 that a writ is enrolled specifically ordering the sheriff of Kent to cause to be made good 'the breaches of the wall of our castle of Rochester which formerly fell.'

Work of this period can still be seen in the curtain wall to the west towards the river and to the south (pages 21, 27), where the projecting DRUM TOWER standing at the junction of the south and east walls is almost certainly of this date and guards the southeast angle of the keep where John's miners had dealt their deadly blow in 1215. It is now known also that the wall to the north of this tower, as far as the first rectangular tower, was realigned at this time before being rebuilt in the fourteenth century.

In the southern curtain wall there was evidently at this period, and perhaps from the beginning, a gateway (page 27). A DRAWBRIDGE and timber defence (BRATTICE) were provided for it in 1224–25, and in 1237 there is direct reference to the repair of 'the gate of that castle towards the south' as well as 'the gate . . . towards the city of Rochester' – that is, the main gate on the east, more or less on the position of the present entrance.

Repairs to the keep (pages 29, 40) evidently began in 1226 with a writ dated 11 March to the sheriff to spend up to £100 on it. Just over a year later, on 18 March 1227, he was ordered to complete what remained to be done, and was credited with an expenditure of about £100 for doing so on his account for Michaelmas in the same year, though floors were laid and the roof leaded as late as 1232.

By this time, therefore, with other miscellaneous buildings within it (including the hall, BUTTERY and DISPENSARY in 1226) also repaired, the castle must have been in as good a condition as before the siege of 1215, and in some respects stronger. Thus in addition to the new drum tower at the southeast angle of the ENCEINTE, there is reference in 1230–31 to the construction of a wall 'in front of the keep' at a cost of over £20 – that is, a wall, now vanished but to which there are later references, dividing the bailey into two parts just north of the keep. Other improvements, both military and residential, were also made to what was clearly one of the major royal castles in the kingdom in the earlier years of Henry III's reign, before it was called upon to resist another destructive siege in 1264.

In 1239 the sheriff was ordered to have the existing chapel plastered, white-washed and decorated with a new painting of Christ in Majesty. In 1244 a new chapel, dedicated to St Margaret, was built in timber adjacent to the royal apartments at a cost of £132;

in 1254 external steps and a new doorway were provided for it to give direct access without the necessity of passing through the King's chamber. Both these chapels in the bailey were WAINSCOTED in 1247, when stained-glass windows, showing armorial bearings and figures of the King, were inserted in the hall.

There were new stables and a new almonry in 1248, and in 1249–50 over £150 were spent on the rebuilding of the main outer gate to the east. In 1256 over £120 were spent upon further repairs to the keep, and in 1258–59, no doubt in response to the political troubles of the kingdom, there was more expenditure upon the keep and the main gate and bridge.

Siege of 1264

The third siege of Rochester occurred at Easter 1264, in the course of the Barons' Wars – a civil war between Henry III and his supporters and a party of magnates led by Earl Simon de Montfort. Rochester was held for the King by Roger de Leybourne, the constable, with John, Earl Warenne, John fitz Alan, Earl of Arundel, Henry of Almain the King's nephew, and others. The siege was begun on 17 April by Gilbert de Clare, Earl of Hertford and Gloucester, advancing from his castle of Tonbridge and evidently attacking from south or west, on the Rochester side of the Medway.

At Earl Gilbert's approach the royalist garrison fired the suburbs towards Canterbury and also, for some reason, the King's hall in the castle. Meanwhile, Earl Simon, with another army, advanced against the city on the other side, from London via Strood. At first he was repulsed at the Medway crossing, but at the third attempt, on Good Friday, 18 April, he got across 'by a certain most subtle device' involving a fire-ship loaded with pitch, coal sulphur and fat bacon – used, it would seem, to fire the bridge, or possibly to

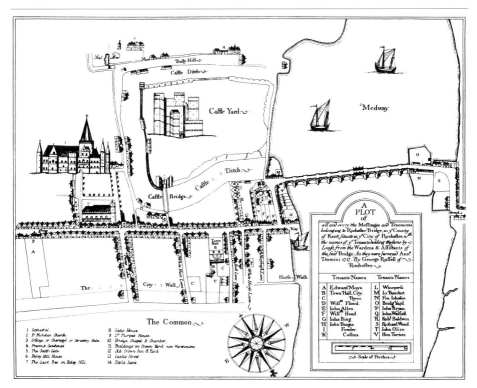

Bridge Warden's map of Rochester in 1717 (from Archaeologia Cantiana *xviii (1896) by permission of the Kent Archaeological Society)*

provide a smoke screen while his forces crossed, presumably by water.

By a previously arranged simultaneous assault from two sides, the two earls entered the city on the same day, 'about the hour of vespers.' Scenes of sacrilege are then reported as men-at-arms rode into the cathedral church in pursuit of fugitives; church valuables were looted and charters and muniments in the prior's chapel destroyed and damaged.

On the next day, Holy Saturday, 19 April, the bailey of the castle was captured, the garrison withdrawing to the keep, as in 1215. On Easter Sunday there was no action, out of respect for religion *(propter solemnitatem)*, but after that the

insurgents turned their siege engines and their arms upon William de Corbeil's great tower. Once more, however, it proved a very hard nut to crack, standing impervious to attack for a whole week. One source claimed that a mine was about to be sprung beneath it, and another that it would have been taken in two more days. In the event it never fell, nor was the matter put to the test, for on Saturday 26 April, Earl Simon and Earl Gilbert abandoned the siege on the news of the advance of the King and his son, the Lord Edward, against them.

The damage done to the fabric of the castle by the siege of 1264 was considerable. Moreover, nothing was done to repair it for just over a century, during which time,

Rochester Castle and bridge in 1809

neglect and wilful damage greatly increased it. Local jurors in 1275, soon after the accession of King Edward I, stated that successive constables and others had stolen materials from the decaying structure for their own use.

In 1281 the then constable, John of Cobham, was given licence to demolish the hall and chambers 'long since burned' (in 1264) and use the stone for constructing other buildings elsewhere in the castle.

A series of surveys taken in the mid fourteenth century, in the reign of Edward III, list serious dilapidations in every quarter of the castle and from top to bottom.

The survey of 1340 is the most useful to historians in listing the buildings and defences of the contemporary fortress. Its purpose was to list the defects in them – in the keep and almost all its component parts, and in the entire circuit of the curtain walls and the cross-wall of the bailey, with their three gates – that is, the south gate 'towards le Boleye,' 'the great outer gate' towards the city, and the inner gate in the cross-wall. The total estimated cost of necessary repairs is put at almost £600, and the jurors state, quite correctly, that the dilapidations began in the time of

Works of 1367–83

Fortunately in Edward III, a warrior, a prodigious builder and a patron of the arts, Rochester Castle had a king prepared to pay for its restoration. Between May 1367 and September 1370 it is known that some £2262 were spent, and the works then completed are sufficiently well documented to indicate that all the recommendations of the detailed survey of 1340 were carried out, as well as certain additions.

The first extant account lists the purchase of a bell from a foundry in London 'to assign the hours to the workmen.' Thereafter there are specific references to the building of whole sections of the curtain walls, to the construction of the two mural towers (page 27) which still stand to the northeast of the keep (one of which was certainly the rebuilding of an earlier tower inserted into Gundulf's wall – page 27), to work upon the inner gate in the cross-wall, and to work upon the great tower or keep, more specifically to its four turrets, its gutters and its lead roof. In addition it is probable that the royal hall and chambers in the bailey were rebuilt at this time. There is reference to the construction of a drawbridge in 1370 (when the main outer gate may have been altered), and considerable further sums were spent on the castle between 1370 and Edward III's death in 1377, though it is not known what was done.

A total sum of over £500 was also spent on Rochester Castle by the government of Richard II. Some of this work was no doubt to make good damage done to the fabric in the Peasants' Revolt of 1381, and some to guard against the possibility of French raids as the war in France went wrong – to repair the castle, as the surviving account expresses it, 'against the damages and dangers imminent from the assaults of the King's enemies.' An important addition to the fortress at this time was the tower or BASTION at its north end towards Rochester

Henry III and had become steadily worse ever since.

A second survey taken in 1363, estimates the cost of repairing the castle at the huge figure of £3333-6s-8d, and a third, dating from 1369, states that the only buildings standing in the castle are the keep, the 'first and second gates,' an old hall with a kitchen and a small stable. Even these were ruined, and so were the walls, and the causes were neglect, a 'great wind' in 1362, and the removal of materials by constables and other officials – 'and so the buildings fell ... until the King thought that measures should be taken to repair the castle.'

Bridge. This bastion was built between 1378 and 1383 (its ruins pierced by the present steps and entrance in about 1872).

Both the castle and city of Rochester must have reached their maximum defensive strength by the end of the fourteenth century. The city walls had been strengthened and repaired in 1344, the fortified area being then slightly extended to the south by a new stretch of wall on the line of the present Prior's Gate of the same date. [For the city walls and defences at Rochester, see G M Livett, 'Medieval Rochester,' in *Archaeologia Cantiana*, xxi (1895), and the plan there printed, with the important modifications and recent survey of Flight and Harrison, *ibid*, lxxxiii, 1968.] Rochester Bridge was rebuilt in stone between 1383 and 1393, with a drawbridge (and a 'wyndynghous' to work it) in the middle, between the sixth and seventh piers. [The medieval bridge crossed the Medway south of the modern bridge on a line marked by the surviving (but restored) Bridge Chapel. Gunpowder was needed to demolish it in 1857. It is clearly shown in the 1717 map of Rochester (page 15). See also M J Becker, *Rochester Bridge 1387–1856* (1930).]

Later history

After the end of the fourteenth century, at least in military terms, the rest is anticlimax, and certainly the architectural development of the castle was at an end.

Although the Clerk of the King's Works is known to have visited Rochester on several occasions towards the middle of the fifteenth century, there are no specific references to any further works at the castle in the medieval period, and in the sixteenth century it was in a state of decay.

In the early seventeenth century James I granted it away from the Crown to Sir Anthony Weldon, in the hands of whose descendants and successors it remained as private property until the late nineteenth century. Meanwhile demolition had been either attempted or suggested in the late eighteenth century, but abandoned because of the difficulty and uneconomic expense of the enterprise. In 1780 there was an abortive proposal to purchase the castle by the government in order to convert it into barracks.

In the 1870s the Corporation of Rochester obtained a lease of the castle grounds from the then owner, Lord Jersey, turned them into a pleasure garden and subsequently acquired the freehold in 1884 for about £6572. This transfer and conversion of the property to public use evidently involved the demolition of the last fragment of the main outer gate, towards the city, and the piercing of a new entrance through the north bastion (above). It also involved, and was followed by, much necessary and valuable work of repair and conservation upon the keep and the curtain wall. In 1965 the Corporation placed the castle in the guardianship of the Ministry of Public Building and Works (later the Department of the Environment). Since 1984 it has been in the care of English Heritage.

DESCRIPTION

Rochester Castle and Cathedral from the northwest, from an engraving by Samuel and Nathaniel Buck, 1735

Bailey

The best view of Rochester Castle, dominated by its majestic keep, is obtained as one approaches from the other, Strood and London, side of the river. From this vantage point the castle and cathedral, standing close together, symbolise (as they were doubtless meant to) the twin pillars of medieval authority – state and church, *regnum* and *sacerdotium*, the two swords, secular and ecclesiastical.

Rochester Castle should be looked at from the outside as well as from the inside. Visitors will find that to walk round the outside is easy and agreeable.

To the northeast all that remains of Gundulf's wall stands as a mutilated fragment of garden wall, with modern wooden gates cut into it, on the far side of the road called Castle Hill, by the County Club, the building of which destroyed more of the medieval wall in the late nineteenth century. The perimeter of the castle grounds to the north and northeast is now bounded by a modern low wall and paling.

Entrances and outer curtain wall

Of the various entrances to the castle at the present time, the two principal ones are from the northeast in Castle Hill (the castle bank has been re-established here) and from the Esplanade through the bastion tower at the northwest angle.

The former entrance more or less occupies the position of the medieval main outer gateway the last traces of which were demolished in 1870–72. It seems likely that the original gateway stood in the same position and was subsequently rebuilt or remodelled, in 1249 or 1250 when some £106 were spent upon the 'repair of the outer gate of the castle,' or as part of Edward III's works in the fourteenth century when the east curtain and its towers were rebuilt (page 17) and a new drawbridge was constructed in 1370. It is shown on the fourteenth-century city seal, on the 1717 map of Rochester (page 15) and on Bucks' view of the castle from the southeast, dated 1735 (page 3). The last, and most detailed, view rather suggests both a fourteenth-century date and that this later work was built in front of Gundulf's entrance to strengthen it (after the manner of the late medieval additions to the early castle gateway at Lewes in Sussex). Much of the gatehouse there shown, comprising the outer entrance archway and its flanking towers or projections, is thrust forward from the curtain wall into the moat, part of which passes under two arches behind it and was doubtless crossed by a drawbridge for greater security. A stone causeway is shown leading to the gate, crossing the moat on arches but with no drawbridge. Part of the causeway and one of its arches were still visible in 1888, but were thereafter obliterated by the building of Castle Hall demolished in 1976.

The present entrance to the castle from the Esplanade at the northwest corner of the castle was cut through the ruins of the fourteenth-century bastion there in or about 1872. The steps and passageway are thus modern and so is the bold 'Norman' archway. On Bucks' view (1735) of the castle from the northwest (page 19) the bastion is shown with its base at the foot of the castle cliff, on the shore of the river, and with a small doorway of which there is now no visible sign.

G T Clark, who evidently saw the ruin of the bastion before its reconstruction and alteration, states that it had a shaft for lifting supplies from the river. [G T Clark, *Mediaeval Military Architecture*, ii, 407.] This shaft was rediscovered during repair work in 1956 and had a blocked doorway facing the river in its otherwise featureless base. It may have served for lifting supplies but may equally have been a GARDEROBE shaft with its doorway for cleaning out. The shaft, now covered over again, is in the westward projection of the bastion near

its junction with the curtain wall. In 1956 traces were also noted of what may have been two NEWEL staircases respectively near each junction, east and west. The bastion itself was built between 1378 and 1383 in the reign of Richard II and stood adjacent to the medieval bridge over the Medway (rebuilt 1382–93) to which in Bucks' view it is joined by a wall (page 19).

The whole stretch of curtain wall along the west or river side of the castle (page 28) – that is, on the right if entering through the bastion, and on the far side of the bailey if entering through the main gate from the city – is basically Gundulf's work of 1087–89, though it rests on Roman foundations and was altered in the thirteenth century. The remains of the Roman city wall, which the Normans utilised here in the construction of their bank and curtain, can be detected at the broken end of this section – that is, towards the bastion – where a subsidence of the cliff revealed them and carried away the medieval wall. From the Esplanade both Roman core and two or three courses of Roman foundation, underpinned by the nineteenth-century REVETMENT of the cliff, can be seen very clearly beneath the eleventh-century wall, itself heightened in the thirteenth century (page 13). [In the words of G M Livett, the nineteenth-century historian of Rochester, 'A finer example of combined Roman, early-Norman and thirteenth-century walling, wisely underpinned in modern times, does not exist in the country' (*Archaeologia Cantiana*, xxi, 33).]

Gundulf's work can be distinguished by the use of uncut stone, frequently laid aslant in either direction in herring-bone fashion to form the facings on the wall, with extra large stones, again uncut, used as internal BUTTRESSES to provide additional strength at any change of direction. The material employed for the facings is Kentish rag, with occasional pieces of tufa and re-used Roman brick, and the core is of rubble, chalk and rag in alternate layers. The original dimensions of Gundulf's wall were a width of some 4¹/₂ft (1.4m) at the base, reduced to 2ft (0.6m) at the summit by offsets in the interior face, and a height of some 22ft (6.7m). Along the top there were CRENELLATIONS, or BATTLEMENTS, which in places can still be seen, though blocked or heightened at a later date with the heightening of the wall.

Against the northernmost part of this section of Gundulf's west curtain, and extending for some 40ft (12m), there are the traces and remains of an important thirteenth-century building, no doubt forming part of the works of Henry III (page 13). Its outer wall (all that remains) abuts against the early-Norman wall, thus thickening it, and oversails it, thus heightening it.

This building was probably a hall, or at least part of a major residential complex in what is the most secure part of the bailey, on the edge of the cliff which formerly rose sheer from the river. It had a VAULTED UNDERCROFT, for three rough pointed arches remain at ground level, though the wall ribs of the vault have been torn away. Above these are the joist holes for the floor of the main upper apartment, of which there also remain (visible from the Esplanade as well as from inside the castle) one and a half window openings, each of two lights, but now blocked. Their arches are slightly depressed, and their material is finely worked and jointed fire-stone (quarried near Reigate and Godstone), characteristic of Henry III's work at Rochester.

This building is followed, to the south, by a crenellated section of the curtain, at the end of which there is a straight joint on the outer face and the wall thickens both externally and internally. While the wall has certainly been at least refaced externally beyond this point, internally its thickening

is evidently to accommodate a series of four EMBRASURES arranged in two pairs, the southern pair being at a higher level than the northern. The embrasures are large and round-headed, and the first three of them each contains a narrow LOOP or window-opening, one-centered and slightly depressed. The fourth and southernmost embrasure contains a much wider opening, now blocked, which from the outside looks like a blocked doorway but was a much ruined two-light window when discovered in the reparations of 1903. [G Payne, 'The Reparation of Rochester Castle,' *Archaeologia Cantiana*, xxvii (1905), page 188.]

Because of their fire-stone dressings all the window-openings are thought to be thirteenth-century piercings of Gundulf's wall, which the 1903 restoration showed to have been thickened on the inside by a new inner face incorporating the embrasures. It is noticeable that here as elsewhere in the castle Henry III's masons followed the round-headed fashion of their Norman predecessors in constructing both the embrasures and the openings, and also that the latter are off-centre in the former.

On the outside, between the third and fourth (blocked) opening, there is a large and elaborate buttress, no longer abutting the wall, also attributed to Henry III's period and containing re-used Roman material. On the inside, just beyond the fourth embrasure and where the wall begins to break away, there is a blocked and shallow arch, springing almost at ground level – evidently a RELIEVING ARCH strengthening Gundulf's curtain where it left the line of the Roman wall to stand on the eleventh-century chalk bank (page 7). The 1903 repairs also revealed, in the centre of the four embrasures just described, traces, now vanished, of the cross-wall that formerly divided the bailey into two. [*Ibid*, page 189.]

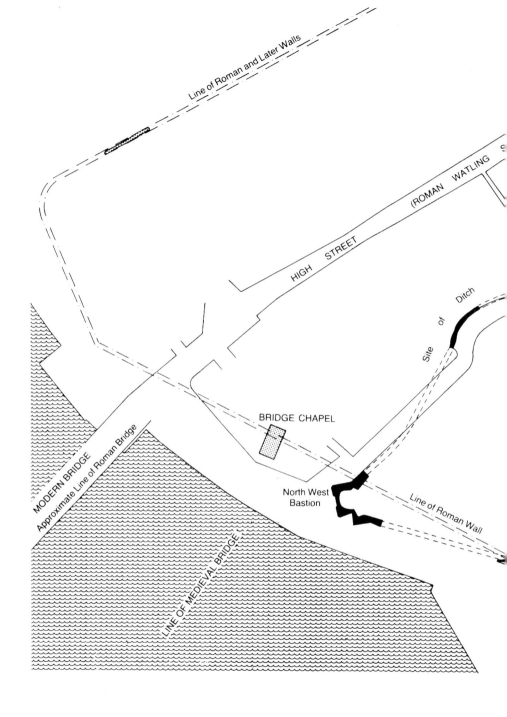

Site plan based on *G M Livett's Map of Medieval Rochester*

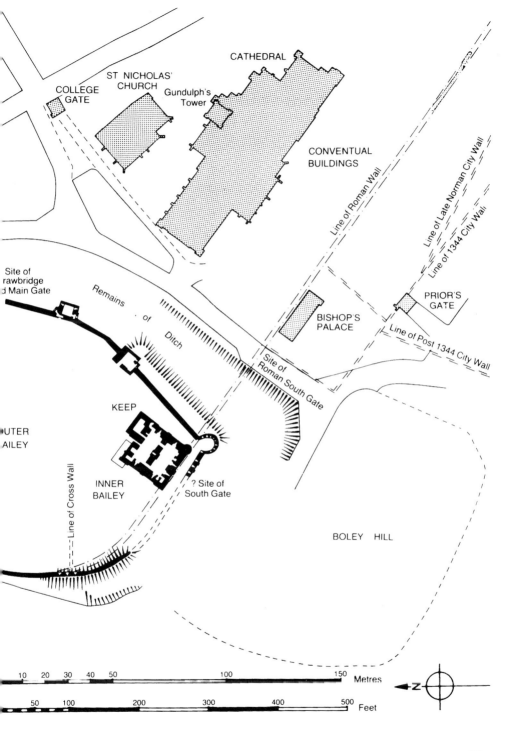

CATHEDRAL

ST NICHOLAS'
CHURCH

COLLEGE
GATE

Gundulph's
Tower

CONVENTUAL
BUILDINGS

Line of Roman Wall

Line of Late Norman City Wall

Line of 1344 City Wall

Site of
rawbridge
d Main Gate

Remains

of

Ditch

PRIOR'S
GATE

BISHOP'S
PALACE

Line of Post 1344 City Wall

Site of
Roman South Gate

KEEP

UTER
AILEY

Line of Cross Wall

INNER
BAILEY

? Site of
South Gate

BOLEY HILL

| 10 | 20 | 30 | 40 | 50 | | 100 | | 150 |

Metres

| 50 | 100 | | 200 | | 300 | | 400 | | 500 |

Feet

Z

23

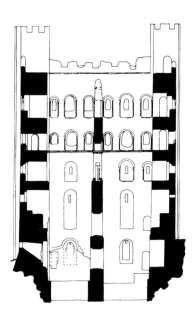

SECTION LOOKING NORTH WEST

SECTION LOOKING SOUTH EAST

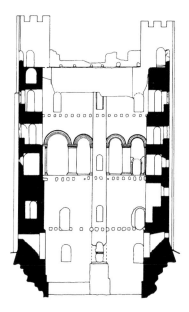

SECTION THROUGH NORTH EAST PART
LOOKING SOUTH WEST

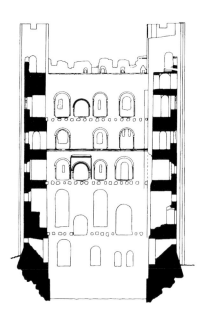

SECTION THROUGH NORTH EAST PART
LOOKING NORTH EAST

Begun 1127   Rebuilt 1226-7

24

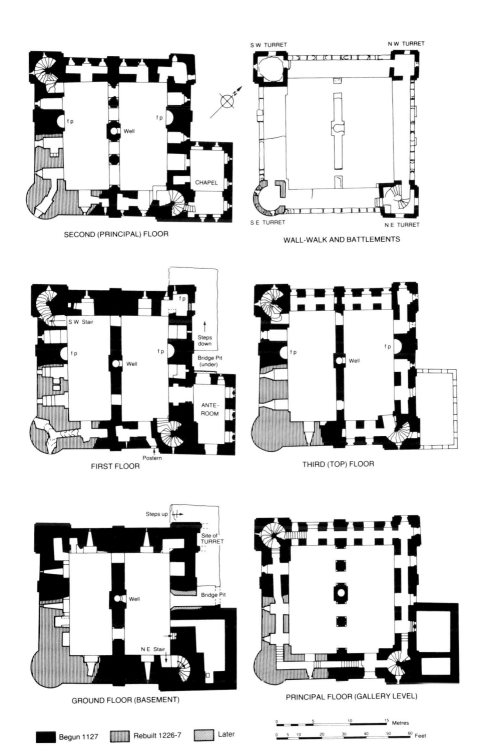

SECOND (PRINCIPAL) FLOOR

f p   f p
Well

CHAPEL

WALL-WALK AND BATTLEMENTS

S W TURRET   N W TURRET

S E TURRET   N E TURRET

FIRST FLOOR

S W Stair

f p   f p
Well

Steps
down

Bridge Pit
(under)

ANTE-
ROOM

Postern

THIRD (TOP) FLOOR

f p   f p
Well

GROUND FLOOR (BASEMENT)

Steps up

Site of
TURRET

Well   Bridge Pit

N E Stair

PRINCIPAL FLOOR (GALLERY LEVEL)

■ Begun 1127   ▨ Rebuilt 1226-7   ▦ Later

0   5   10   15 Metres
0 5 10   20   30   40   50   60 Feet

25

The castle from the Medway

(right) Entrance cut through Edward III's bastion in 1872 to give access to the new pleasure gardens in the bailey. The arch is decorated in the style of the much older arches in the keep

South and southeast curtain wall and Henry III's southeast tower

In the vicinity of the embrasures and openings described above, the early-Norman curtain left the line of the Roman city wall, which turns inside it to run under the southern face of the keep (see the site plan on pages 22–3). A long section of Gundulf's wall, from the southwest angle along the south of the castle enclosure, has been destroyed in modern times; the low retaining wall which replaces it and marks its line is Corporation work of the late nineteenth century.

Next comes a length of some 50ft (15m) of curtain wall, pierced by a line of arrow loops (splayed internally and with slightly depressed heads) which evidently formed a shooting gallery at this point. At the west end of this length of wall, where it is broken away, there is a vertical CHACE on both the inner and outer faces, which may mark the site of the former southern gate of the castle (page 14).

At the east end of the wall is a rounded and projecting mural tower of two stages, its lower stage of arrow loops corresponding in height to those of the shooting gallery in the wall. The tower is of early thirteenth-century style, and both it and the adjacent curtain just described are generally considered part of the post-war repairs of Henry III's reign (page 13), designed both to close the breach in the castle enclosure torn by King John's miners (page 11) and to strengthen a position that had been shown to be vulnerable. Wall and tower join, however, in so clumsy a fashion that they cannot possibly be of one build and date, and as one of the shooting embrasures of the wall appears to have been broken off to effect the juncture, it seems likely that the wall was built first. The tower measures some 30ft (9m) in diameter and is splayed out at the base to the field. Much of its outer face has at some time been renewed; internally it had two storeys with timber floors, and was probably always open to the GORGE as it is now.

Finally, recent excavation has shown that the section of curtain running north from this southeast cylindrical tower to the rectangular tower north of it was also rebuilt on a new alignment at this time.

Edward III's east curtain wall and mural towers
The whole length of curtain along the east side of the castle, from Henry III's drum tower northwards to the site of the former main gateway (which may also have been remodelled at this time – page 14), and including the two rectangular mural towers which stand upon it, are the work of Edward III and date from 1367–70 (page 17).

Here, on the outside, visitors may gain some impression of the width of the moat, which formerly surrounded the castle on the three landward sides (page 4), though much of its depth is now filled in. Also from the vicinity of Henry III's tower, the best view can be obtained of the cylindrical southeast angle of the keep, rebuilt in this shape after the siege of 1215 (page 11), as well as the extent of the damage done by John's miners. The latter is especially evident on the south face of the keep where, almost half-way across, the fissure is plainly visible, and the damaged remains of one of the decorated windows of the top stage, blocked and not rebuilt, can be seen.

Between Henry III's drum tower and the southernmost of Edward III's rectangular towers (that nearest the keep) the inner bank of the moat has been shored up by a brick retaining wall. From the latter tower northwards, however, this bank has long since fallen away (cf Bucks' view of 1735) and this with more recent investigations has revealed the foundations of both the wall and the two rectangular towers of Edward III. By contrast to the northern tower, which is all of one build, the southern tower (now underpinned) is known to stand upon earlier foundations of mortared rubble, most probably of twelfth-century date, and thus to be the fourteenth-century rebuilding of an early mural tower inserted into Gundulf's, curtain after the latter was built. As a further distinction, it may also be noted that this southern tower straddles the wall whereas the northern one is entirely projecting to the field.

The foundations of Edward III's curtain wall are remarkable for their somewhat unusual employment of 'arches of

West curtain wall

construction,' four of which can be seen between the two towers, roughly fashioned and not, of course, intended to show. The stone used for the facings of the wall and the facings and dressings of the towers is Kentish rag from the Boughton quarries.

The towers themselves are each of two storeys and boldly splayed externally by BATTERS towards the field. The southern tower (nearest the keep) is now used for storage. It had timber flooring, now vanished, and an external staircase turret. There are few notable features. Its northern fellow is more elaborate and must have been intended for residential purposes. Converted in modern times into a cottage, it has a fine fourteenth-century

vault, a stone VICE, and traces of former garderobes.

Between the two towers an opening has been hacked through the wall in modern times, evidently to provide a view of the cathedral; its lower half is now blocked, presumably for reasons of safety.

Northwards from the northern tower, Edward III's curtain wall runs on, with its re-established bank, almost to the site of the former main gate, finally demolished in 1870–72 (page 18). Beyond this again, on the other side of Castle Hill (as described on pages 4 and 7) there survives the mutilated northeast fragment of Gundulf's wall, which formerly ran along the north side of the bailey to Richard II's bastion at the northwest angle (page 17).

Eastern mural tower rebuilt by Edward III (1367–70) on the site of an earlier, twelfth-century tower

Keep

The keep (in contemporary parlance the donjon) was not only the military strongpoint but also contained the most lordly accommodation. It is in every way the most outstanding feature in Rochester Castle. It stands at the southern end of the bailey close by the curtain wall, and was built by Archbishop William de Corbeil in the earlier twelfth century (about 1127; see page 8).

Uncompromisingly rectangular, except for the rebuilt southeastern angle, the keep measures some 70ft (21m) square externally at ground level, with a PLINTH or splayed-out base. It rises to a height of some 113ft (34m) to the top of the parapet, with the four angle turrets rising a further 12ft (3.7m) above that. Rectangular holes for fitting a

timber HOARDING or brattice round the top still show beneath the battlements, especially on the east face and southeast angle.

Built chiefly of Kentish rag, with ASHLAR dressings and QUOINS from Caen in Normandy, its walls have a width of some 12ft (3.7m) at the base, narrowing to l0ft (3m) at the summit by means of a slight external batter, their immense thickness facilitating the construction of numerous mural chambers and galleries, as at the contemporary tower at Castle Hedingham in Essex or the later twelfth-century tower at Dover in Kent.

Except in the rebuilt southeast section (where the original structure presumably conformed with the rest) the walls are further strengthened at each corner by a pair of PILASTER buttresses, nooked at their angles and rising above the PARAPET to form the corner turrets. This arrangement is slightly complicated at the northeast corner by the presence of the forebuilding, and the southeast corner has been replaced by the thirteenth-century cylindrical rebuilding. There is also a flat pilaster buttress near the centre of each side of the tower, and on the north face a second formed by continuing the west wall of the forebuilding upwards. The whole tower is given an even greater structural rigidity by means of an internal, east – west, crosswall that divides it from top to bottom.

The internal arrangement of the keep was a basement at ground level with three residential floors above it. The second and principal residential floor was formed of two stages thrown together (again as at Hedingham) to provide greater height and spaciousness, with a mural gallery at the second stage to provide more light. This arrangement of the various floors and stages is marked externally by the lines of window-openings and loops, which for obvious reasons of security and defences are small at the lower levels of the tower and increase to the large and handsome size of the two upper lines marking the mural gallery of the second floor and the third floor respectively.

Externally, only the top stage of windows – those of the third floor – were decorated, with HALF-SHAFTS, CAPITALS and CHEVRON-ornamented arches, though this elaboration was not repeated in the rebuilt section of the keep. Except those at first-floor level which are square headed, all the window-openings are round headed. All were single lights except the two-light windows of the entrance vestibule at first-floor level in the forebuilding, and the larger of the window openings in the main tower at second-floor gallery level (the penultimate stage) which were also originally of two lights, though now much

broken away. There are also, generally near the angles, numerous miscellaneous loops (those at the top stage having originally been decorated in conformity with the other windows of that floor) marking stairways, mural chambers and garderobes. Each angle turret has a plain single-light window-opening on each of its outer faces.

Forebuilding, entrance vestibule and chapel

Unlike the earliest Norman keeps in England at Colchester and the Tower of London, but in common with most contemporary and later twelfth-century great towers, Rochester was provided with an elaborate forebuilding (on its north face) and other defensive arrangements to guard its entrance.

This entrance, recently reopened, is placed at first-floor level on the north face of the keep. It is reached by an external staircase which began on the west (river) side of the keep against the northwest angle buttresses and turns the northwest angle through the lower stage of a small tower now almost entirely vanished. The ramp of this staircase remains and upon it modern steps have now been laid so that visitors can enter the keep as their forebears did.

The small tower at the northwest angle, the principal purpose of which was to block and guard the staircase at an intermediate level and cover it in both directions with superior shooting-power, stood some 12ft (3.7m) square, flush with the west face of the keep and projecting to the north. It rose through two vaulted stages, its second floor communicating with the so-called Gundulf's Chamber in the northwest corner of the first floor of the keep, through a doorway now blocked. The two arches marking the vaults of each floor, the blocked doorway between them, and the SPRINGER of the outer archway through which the staircase passed, are still visible on the north face of the keep.

From here the original staircase ramp (some 8ft or 2.4m broad and formerly protected by an outer parapet) and modern steps ascend the north front of the keep to the forebuilding proper. This, again, covered the staircase by its superior shooting-power, and was entered via a drawbridge (now replaced by a fixed bridge) across a drawbridge pit some 15ft (4.6m) deep and 9ft (2.7m) wide. At the bottom of the pit an entrance has at some date been hacked into the basement of the keep (another through the north face of the forebuilding was until recently visitors' entrance to the keep).

On the far side of the bridge and in the west face of the forebuilding the original doorway through which visitors enter is very grand, 6ft (1.8m) wide with a round arch decorated by chevron moulding and flanked inside and out by ENGAGED COLUMNS with plain capitals. The drawbar holes for the closing of the door are still visible on either side.

The entrance vestibule to which access is thus gained was also an impressive apartment, the anteroom of archbishops and sometimes kings. Measuring 26ft (8m) in length and 14ft (4.3m) across its widest (west) end, it had originally five round-headed windows, of which four remain – one of a single light to the west beside the entrance, three, each of two lights, along the north wall on the left, and one, slightly larger, in the east wall, again presumably of two lights but having been converted into a POSTERN doorway at some later date. Floor and ceiling were and are of timber (now a modern replacement) except that the narrower east end of the room has a BARREL-VAULTED ceiling to carry the stone floor of the CHANCEL of the chapel above.

Immediately to the right as one enters is the entrance to the keep itself, even grander than the entrance from the outside stairway. The round arch has bold chevron ornament, and the 6ft 2in (1.9m) opening

Northwest view of the keep, with the forebuilding on left, before the recent restoration of the entrance

is flanked on either side by NOOK SHAFTS. The wall of the keep here, through which this entrance passes, is 10ft 6in (3.2m) thick. The door was secured not only by a drawbar, but also by a PORTCULLIS, the grooves for which can still be seen. Behind the rebate of the door on either side of the passage at its inner end, there is a small round-headed recess, conceivably for lamps.

The entrance vestibule just described gives access to the keep at first-floor level but is itself the third of the four floors or stages of the forebuilding, all of which it is convenient to describe here before the keep.

Built against the eastern half of the north face of the great tower, the forebuilding rises to about two-thirds of its height and has a crenellated roof. Above the entrance vestibule, in the top storey, there is a handsome chapel that was designed to be *en suite* with the second and principal residential stage of the keep, but can no longer be reached from it as that once noble building now lacks all its floors. It is entered instead through a forced opening, with steps up into its chancel, off the northeast vice or spiral staircase (page 38). It measures 28ft (8.5m) by some 15ft (4.6m), narrowing slightly from west to east, and is divided by a bold round-headed arch of 12ft (3.7m) span into two parts forming chancel and NAVE and comprising respectively one-third and two-thirds of the whole. There are seven recessed and round-headed windows in all, two at the east end, two at the west end, and three in the north wall (one in the chancel and two in the nave).

The chancel has a half-octagonal vault and a modern stone floor which rests on the barrel vault of the east end of the entrance vestibule beneath. Behind the presumed position of the altar there is a

Main entrance to the keep from the forebuilding, formerly protected by a portcullis that was lowered from above in the grooves that can be seen

drain through the east wall, and to the right of this there is a deep and wide recess which was probably a SEDILIA but has been hacked through to make the rough, stepped passage from the spiral staircase by which visitors now enter. The nave has a modern timber floor reproducing the original at the correct level, and a modern roof. The holes for the rafters of the original twelfth-century roof are raked, showing that it was pitched, though its summit would not have risen above the battlemented tops of the forebuilding walls. There are signs that at a later date, perhaps in Edward III's time, this arrangement was heightened and altered to a flat roof at the same level as the summit of the original one.

The proper entrance into the chapel is in the south wall of the nave towards the west end. It is a tall round-headed doorway $3^{1}\!/_{2}$ft (1m) wide, opening into a wider passage that leads into the second-floor apartments of the keep. Immediately outside the chapel doorway are the groove and chace, and on either side a recess for the windlass of the portcullis which closed the entrance into the keep on the floor beneath, and which must have been somewhat inconveniently worked from this position which thus served both as a portcullis chamber and the chapel entrance.

Basements of forebuilding
Beneath the entrance vestibule of the forebuilding there are two further floors or basements. The lower of these presents problems of interpretation. In plan it consists of two adjoining rectangles, the larger, to the west, measuring some 14ft (4.3m) square and the smaller, to the east, some 10ft (3m) square. It is vaulted throughout. Originally it could be reached only by a narrow passageway and steps leading down from the basement of the keep itself; this entrance being the only means of lighting and ventilation apart from a garderobe shaft descending into it at its

east end from the room above. The steps terminate 11 ft 6in (3.5m) above an earthen floor. This basement is known to have been dug out to this depth at the beginning of the twentieth century, and therefore its original depth is uncertain. [George Payne, 'The Reparation of Rochester Castle,' *Archaeologia Cantiana*, xxvii (1905), page 185.] It remains possible that the existing earthen floor roughly corresponds with the twelfth-century one as the faces of the walls, while descending to so great a depth, do not look as though they have been buried over a long period, and because at the present floor level, at the east end of this subterranean apartment, there are traces of a cross-wall which must have been a retaining wall for the cesspit of the garderobe discharging from the upper basement above.

Described in some of the older literature on Rochester as a dungeon – in the modern sense of a deep, dark and dismal prison – it seems likely that this underground chamber may have been chiefly used as a combined cesspit and rubbish dump, and it is certain that there is no authentic evidence for the incarceration of prisoners within it.

Above this, the upper basement of the forebuilding, immediately below the entrance vestibule the timber floor of which formed its ceiling, has the same shape and dimensions as the lower one. It, too, was (and still is) reached only by a passageway from the basement of the keep itself, in this case sloping up through the north wall of the keep which is here 11 ft (3.4m) thick. Used, no doubt, chiefly for storage, it was lit and ventilated by two air shafts, one through its east wall and one through its north, visible just below the joist holes of the ceiling. In its east wall there was also a garderobe recess, later widened, the shaft of which discharged into the cesspit in the lower basement.

Plan and construction of main tower
The recent restoration of the original entrance to the keep via the entrance

vestibule of the forebuilding means that visitors enter the main tower correctly at first-floor level (page 30). Here, however, they find themselves standing upon a mere modern timber platform and may well pause to take stock. A considerable effort of the imagination is required to recall the original arrangements, and the former grandeur, of what was a lordly fortified residence of the twelfth-century Archbishops of Canterbury, who built and kept it.

At some date, unrecorded but presumably in the post-medieval period, the whole of the interior was burnt out. Much of the masonry was charred pink and was found, during repairs, to be spattered with lead from the roof. The roof and all the timber floors are missing. The unhappy absence of these, however, enables the whole of the building to be taken in at a glance, or rather, one half of it at a time, for the keep is divided from top to bottom by the cross-wall, pierced at the level of the principal residential apartments, on the second floor, by an ARCADE of stout Romanesque columns of unequal size and span. The well-shaft is situated near the centre of this cross-wall, and was ingeniously carried up through it, with a well-head on every floor, facing north in each case.

The internal arrangement of the keep, a basement and three self-contained residential suites, is sufficiently indicated by the joist holes of the floors and by the levels of the doorways and window openings. The present level of the earthen floor of the basement is thus wrong and misleading. There being no joist holes, the basement must always have had an earth floor, the true level of which – some 14ft (4.3m) higher and more or less on the level of another timber platform supplied at that level – is clearly shown by the doors and windows now, as it were, suspended in mid air. It was dug out to its existing depth at the beginning of the twentieth century, though even so the bottom of the walls was still not found. [Payne,

Arcade at principal floor level of the keep. The well-head is shown in the centre

Well-head at first-floor level, as rebuilt in 1826. The well-shaft continued upwards with access at each floor level

Archaeologia Cantiana, xxvii (1905), pages 184–5.]

These facts afford some insight into the method of construction of the keep, for the depth of the foundations was prodigious, and the walls appear to have been laid in foundation trenches up to the level of the rough offset still visible. Once they had been carried up further, the whole interior of the tower must have been filled up with rammed earth to the required level of the earthen basement floor. The object would be the achievement of structural rigidity for so great a mass of masonry and a defence against undermining. Hence the achievement of King John's miners in bringing down one quarter of the fabric in

1215 (page 11) appears even more formidable.

Communication between all levels of the keep from roof to basement was provided by a broad stone VICE (spiral staircase) in the northeast angle, on the left, and by another, similar, in the opposite southwest angle which, however, never descended to basement level and is now much ruined.

Ground floor or basement

The basement itself, like every storey of the keep, is divided by the cross-wall into two nearly equal parts, each 46ft (14m) long with widths of 21ft (6.4m) in the north part and 20ft (6m) in the south. It was originally entered only from the main northeast spiral staircase leading down into its northern half, and there a modern timber platform is supplied for visitors.

The northern apartment was lit by three narrow round-headed loops, one in the west wall, one in the east wall, and one in the north, just clear of the forebuilding and opening into the drawbridge pit. This last loop has at some late date been hacked out into an entrance, now blocked by an iron grating. All three loops are or were set deep in a double recess – the outer recess splayed, and the inner recess flat-sided and descending to the floor.

In the north wall, east of the former loop now converted into an entrance, are two narrow doorways – one, the eastern-most, leading down seven steps to the lower basement of the forebuilding, the other leading up an incline in the upper basement of the forebuilding, both previously described. Also in the north wall, west or left of the hacked entrance, there is a recess some 6ft (1.8m) square, and beyond this again, in the west wall near the junction of the west and north walls, there is a broken doorway leading into a small mural chamber or compartment, featureless but corresponding in its position in the northwest angle to the mural chambers of

the residential floors above.

The well-head (restored and dated 1826) is in the centre of the cross-wall on its northern face, and on either side of it, asymmetrically placed, is a doorway opening through the cross-wall into the southern compartment.

The southern half of the basement was lit by four loops, one to the west, one to the east (now blocked), and two in the south wall, all round-headed and deeply recessed in the same manner as those in the northern half. In the southwest angle there is a small featureless mural chamber very much like that in the northwest angle in the other half of the basement. The southeast angle, whatever its original arrangement may have been, was rebuilt solid in the early thirteenth-century repairs to the keep which followed the siege of 1215. Immediately west or right of the southeast angle, and in the south wall, there is a rectangular recess some 6ft (1.8m) wide and 3ft (0.9m) deep. To the right of this recess, between it and the adjacent loop, and also in the west wall to the right of the southwest angle, there are rough openings which have at some date been hacked through into the vertical shafts serving garderobes on the upper floors.

The whole of the basement area, including its various recesses and mural chambers or compartments, was probably intended principally for storage.

First floor

The first floor, reached from the basement only by the northeast vice, is divided by the cross-wall into two parts, of similar dimensions to those below, and which probably served as hall and great chamber respectively. Communication between them was given by two doorways placed asymmetrically east and west in the crosswall. In the western doorway remains of a jamb and REBATE for a door can still be seen. The cross-wall also contains, as on every floor, a round-headed well-head near its centre, facing north.

Though the interpretation of medieval domestic arrangements is hazardous, it is probable that the whole of this floor, which is also the floor of entry to the keep from the vestibule in the forebuilding, was assigned to the resident constable, as distinct from the lord of the castle or his lordly guests. It is clear from the fireplaces and garderobes provided that the accommodation was intended for a person of some consequence.

The main northern apartment (hall?) was entered direct from outside, via the external staircase and entrance vestibule, or from the northeast spiral staircase. There are four window embrasures, two in the north wall, west of the vestibule entrance and with a fireplace between them, and one placed centrally in both the west and east walls. The loops are, or were, square-headed (that between the fireplace and the vestibule entrance is blocked) and, except for the more complicated arrangement of the eastern embrasure, were set back in deep, plain round-headed recesses 15ft (4.6m) high. At their lower levels, however, these recesses have been reduced in depth by later blocking, presumably to strengthen the walls which they were weakening.

The eastern window embrasure has the loop placed high and centrally within it to accommodate a passage opening off it to the south, leading to a ventilated garderobe the shaft of which opens externally on the east face of the keep, and, on its left, a postern cut obliquely through the wall and opening on the east front of the keep near the forebuilding, some 15ft (4.5m) up from the ground. The draw-bar holes of the postern door can still be seen, and it must presumably have communicated by a wooden bridge with the wallwalk of the curtain some 30ft (9m) away. The fireplace between the two northern window recesses is round-headed with a round back and a

conical flue leading up to a lateral vent in the north wall.

In the northwest corner of the keep, with its round-headed entrance in the west wall of this apartment left of the angle, there is a pleasant mural chamber, the so-called *Gundulf's Chamber*, which was probably the private room of the constable. It is vaulted and GROINED, with two recessed window loops to the west, a hooded fireplace in its rounded northwest angle and, in the north wall, a blocked doorway that led to the upper storey of the small tower which commanded the external entrance staircase at this angle of the keep.

The main southern apartment (the great chamber?) of this first-floor level is entered either through the doorways in the cross-wall or from the southwest vice which descends to this level but no further. It had five plain round-headed window embrasures, one in the west wall, three in the south and one in the east. The loops are square-headed and set back in deep, tall recesses like those of the northern apartment and similarly partly blocked at their lower levels. The west window recess and the centre window recess of the three in the south wall each had a garderobe opening off from the left jamb (and using the shafts that are broken into on the basement floor below). The window recess in the east wall similarly has a passageway or recess, which may once have been a garderobe, opening off its left jamb, and to the right or south a passage running into the rebuilt southeast angle where it divides and terminates in two arrow loops.

The fireplace of the southern apartment is of the same pattern as the fireplace in the northern, and is correspondingly situated in the south wall between the two easternmost of the three southern window recesses.

Second or principal floor

There is every indication that the second floor, entered from both the northeast and southwest vices contained the state apartments and the grandest residential suite. The two principal apartments north and south of the cross-wall were given a lofty height of some 27ft (8m) by combining two stages of the tower, a moulded STRING-COURSE marking the division. There are two tiers of windows, roughly corresponding, the recesses of the upper tier piercing a MURAL GALLERY which surrounds this floor on all four sides. Further spaciousness and grandeur was achieved by piercing the cross-wall at this level by an arcade (page 34), stout Norman columns and half-columns (the central pier accommodating the well-head) with SCALLOPED capitals, supporting arches of unequal size and richly moulded with roll-and-hollow and chevron decoration. Into this arcade a stone screen some 10ft (3m) high was evidently fitted (but not bonded in), of which a fragment including an almost complete round-headed doorway (with a rebate for the door), survives within the westernmost arch.

In matters of detail also the finishing and decorations of this floor were more elaborate than those of the floor below and the floor above. The two fireplaces of the main apartments each have a handsome chevron ARCHITRAVE set in a rectangular projecting chimneypiece; the openings of doors and windows have half-shafts and decorated round arches (roll-and-hollow moulding in the lower tier and chevron in the upper); at this level alone in the keep the buttress projection of the well in the cross-wall is flanked by nook-shafts.

The main northern apartment (hall?) has at its lower stage one window recess in the west wall and one in the east, with two in west end of the north wall, the fireplace standing between them. This is the same arrangement as on the floor below, but everywhere on this second floor the loops themselves, at the back of these deep recesses, were more elaborately framed

except in the rebuilt southeast corner. The east and west window recesses here have each a passageway opening at right-angles from the southern jamb and leading to what is certainly in the eastern recess a garderobe lit by a single loop.

The well-head, as on every floor of the keep, opens into this northern apartment. In the northwest corner there is a doorway in the west wall giving access to a private mural chamber corresponding to Gundulf's Chamber on the first floor below it. This has a window facing west another, now much broken away, to the north, and again a fireplace between them in the rounded northwest angle.

In the north wall of the main apartment, to the right or east of the two windows with the fireplace between them, and situated above the entrance from the forebuilding on the first floor below it, there is a fine doorway, with a roll-and-hollow moulded arch almost 8ft (2.4m) wide. This opens into a passageway which after some 9ft (2.7m) is reduced by a rebate to $3^{1/2}$ft (1m) to form the doorway to the chapel (page 31).

The main southern apartment (great chamber?) on this second floor, like the corresponding apartment on the first floor, communicates with the southwest vice. It has a deep window embrasure to west and east, and three in its south wall with an elaborate fireplace (of the same pattern as its fellow in the northern apartment) between the western two. The western window embrasure branches out at right-angles to north and south into two recesses – of which the southern is certainly a garderobe – each lit by a single loop (thus making a group of three loops). The eastern recess similarly has a passageway from its northern jamb leading to what may have been a garderobe with a loop. There is also a garderobe with no loop in the left jamb of the window embrasures on the left of the fireplace.

The mural gallery, barrel vaulted, runs round the entire second floor at its upper level. It passes through the angle turrets and the two spiral staircases, occasionally altering its level slightly by steps to accommodate the stairs, the abutment of the cross-wall and the rebuilt southeast angle, and is traversed by the window embrasures.

The actual window openings of these embrasures are very much broken away, and in any case the original arrangements were not reproduced in the rebuilt southeast section of the keep. It appears that while some were smaller single-light openings, others, symmetrically arranged and in wider embrasures, were larger two-light openings, and that these included the centre window of each group of three in the west wall, the window in the east wall of the northern half of the keep (where traces of a two-light opening can be detected), and the two outer windows of the three in the south wall. This original arrangement survives in only one instance: in the handsome two-light window, stepped up to clear the chapel roof, with round moulded arches, stout Norman column and half-shafts and scalloped capitals, at the east end of the northern gallery. Sheltered by the forebuilding and evidently blocked up when the chapel roof was raised, it was discovered and reopened in 1899. [Payne, *Archaeologia Cantiana*, xxvii (1905), page 18]. All the original windows at this gallery level have slots for draw-bars for securing their shutters.

Third floor

From the second floor and its mural gallery, both the southwest and northeast spiral stairs led up to the top floor of the keep, with a passage leading off the latter on to the roof of the forebuilding.

The third and highest residential floor was only slightly less grand than the main second floor below. The round-headed fireplaces (page 39), window embrasures and doorways are decorated with chevron ornament, except in the rebuilt southeast corner, and the window openings, of generous proportions and fitted originally with draw-bar holes for their shutters, are, with the same exception, decorated with half-shafts and chevron ornament, externally. The cross-wall, now broken down but still containing the well shaft brought up to this level with the well-head to the north, was solid here and not arcaded as on the second floor, but its two doorways, east and west, between the two main apartments, evidently had rebates for doors.

The whole floor occupied only one stage of the keep, but each apartment had a height of 19ft (5.8m) beneath a timber roof, and was provided with mural galleries which do not pass behind the cross-wall, nor behind the fireplaces (because of their lateral vents), and are absent from the southeast corner (presumably because of its rebuilding).

The main northern apartment (hall?) thus had three handsome window embrasures in the west wall overlooking the river, interconnected by a gallery which, to the north, does not pass into the northwest angle and, to the south, terminates in a shallow recess against the cross-wall. To the east are two window embrasures plus the entrance from the northeast vice, again all interconnected by a gallery terminating in a shallow recess in the cross-wall to the south. In the north wall there are also three embrasures, one on either side of the fireplace and a third further east. That to the left of the fireplace has a gallery or passageway leading off at right-angles from its left jamb into a small square chamber in the northwest angle, with windows to north and west (but no fireplace). This corresponds in position to the chambers in this angle at every other level of the keep. The two embrasures east of the fireplace are again connected by a

Interior of the southeast corner of the keep. The incomplete arch on the left shows where Henry III's masons repaired the breach caused when this corner of the keep was undermined by King John

gallery which also traverses the easternmost embrasure to form a blind passageway or closet out of its eastern jamb.

The southern apartment of this top floor is in some ways the most interesting part of the keep. Its basic layout is similar to that of its northern fellow and to that of the corresponding southern apartment on the second floor. There are three window embrasures in the west wall, interconnected by a gallery which does not enter the southwest angle and terminates to the north in a recess in the cross-wall. In the south wall there are, in addition to the entrance from the southwest staircase, three window recesses, one west of the fireplace and two to the east. In the east wall there is one window embrasure only. However, at this level, better than anywhere else, the great fissure torn by John's miners in 1215, and the thirteenth-century reparations which followed, can be seen. They extend from just left of the fireplace round the southeast angle to a point some two-thirds of the way to the cross-wall.

Everywhere, at this level as below it, although Henry III's masons followed the twelfth-century fashion of their predecessors in rebuilding round-headed arches and embrasures, the work was done crudely, without regard to previous decoration and embellishments. Thus immediately left of the fireplace at this top-storey level, one can see the remains of an original decorated window embrasure, not renewed but replaced by one smaller and perfectly plain, like its fellow further east in the same wall. Most notable – and again replaced by a smaller, plain embrasure – is the survival in the east wall of nearly half of a large and fine arch of two roll-moulded ORDERs resting upon two half-shafts with a sculptured and a CUSHION CAPITAL respectively. The scale and embellishment of this arch, unlike anything else in the keep, and its ecclesiastical appearance, suggest its interpretation as

the recess for the east window and altar of a chapel.

The fact that the great tower of Rochester was built by Archbishop William de Corbeil, and symbolised the lordship of the archbishops as perpetual custodians of the castle, would seem sufficient to account for the placing of a large chapel in this somewhat unusual position, occupying at least the eastern part of the south half of the keep at this level. If so, the tower of Rochester, with this chapel housed within it as well as the lesser chapel in the forebuilding, may be thought to stand, as it were, halfway between the unique design of the earlier towers of Colchester and London, with their apsidal chapels worked into their fabric, and the more usual plan of later twelfth-century keeps with one or more chapels in the forebuilding only. It may also follow that at Rochester this highest residential floor contained the private accommodation of the archbishop.

Wallwalk and turrets

Access to the wallwalk at the summit of the tower was originally by either of the spiral staircases, though now only by the northeast. On the way up, a passage from this opens into a gallery in the east wall, traversed by a window embrasure which, internally, opened into the gable of the northern apartment of the top floor.

The wallwalk is almost continuous, passing through each of the angle turrets except the southwest where it is blocked by the turret's eastern wall. The turret-chambers through which one passes are some 8ft (2.4m) high and have two loops or windows, one in each outer face towards the field. Above this their upper levels must have been reached by ladders. The wallwalk had a RERE-WALL some 3ft (0.9m) high, now vanished, and the outer battlemented parapet stood 8ft (2.4m) high with five MERLONS to each section between the turrets. At the foot of the parapet there can still be seen in many places the holes for the timber joist to support the hoarding or brattice – a projecting timber gallery used for defending the base of the tower in time of war – which was reached by openings, now blocked, in the centre of each section.

From the wallwalk one can also see (as well as a splendid view in all directions) the arrangement and line of the missing roof, a double one, low (but unequally) pitched above each half of the keep, the ridges not rising above the battlements, with a common central gutter along the top of the cross-wall and side gutters to north and south. At this high level the great tower of Rochester also gives one other glimpse of medieval domestic economy. Along the inner face of the north wall, between the summit and the roof line, there is a double row of pigeon holes, and many others, now blocked, were originally provided in the turrets – the castellated equivalent of the dovecotes still found on some old farms and manors.

Glossary

Arcade   Series of arches on columns or piers

Architrave   Lowest division of the entablature; ornamental band round a door or corridor opening

Bailey   Walled enclosure or courtyard of a castle

Ashlar   Squared hewn stone laid in regular courses with fine vertical joints

Barrel vault   Continuous arched vault of semicircular section

Bastion   Projection from the general outline of a fortress from which the garrison can see, and defend by flanking fire, the ground before the ramparts

Batter   Inclined face of a wall

Battlements   Indented parapet; crenellation

Brattice   See *Hoarding*

Buttery   Storeroom where drink (especially ale), butter, cheese, bread and other provisions were kept and issued

Buttress   Masonry built against a wall to give additional support

Capital   Uppermost part of a column or shaft, often decorated

Chancel   Eastern part of a church, generally divided from the nave by a screen or railing (*cancellus*)

Chase   Groove or channel cut into the face of a wall or floor to receive a pipe, beam, drain, etc

Chevron   Architectural ornament in the form of an inverted V

Claustral   Pertaining to cloisters

Cloisters   Four-sided enclosure between monastic buildings and the church with a covered walk or alley along each side; the centre of monastic life

Crenellation   Battlements

Curtain wall   Wall enclosing a castle or one of its parts

Cushion capital   Cubic capital with lower angles rounded off to fit a circular shaft

Dispensary   Place in which medicines were dispensed; room for the relief of the sick poor

Donjon   Keep; great tower

Drawbridge   Wooden bridge which can be raised towards a gateway by ropes or chains attached to its outer end

Drum tower   Low round tower

Embrasure   Splayed opening in a wall for admitting light or shooting through

Enceinte   Main line of towers and curtain walls, as distinct from outworks

Engaged column   Column attached to or partly sunk into a wall

Entablature   Horizontal member above a classic column, often used with the column. It consists of three parts: the upper projecting cornice; the frieze, which when it swells outwards is said to by pulvinated; and the lower member, the architrave, which may be used as a frame for window, door or fireplace openings

Fief   Land or estate granted (and inherited) by feudal tenure in 'fee' or return for service

Garderobe   Latrine, normally discharging into a cesspit or through an outer wall into the moat or onto the berm (the space between the base of the wall and the moat)

Gorge   Rear entrance, whether open or closed, of any outwork

Groin   Edge formed by the intersection of two vaults

Half shaft   Half a column (halved vertically) attached to a wall

Hoarding   Hoard/hourd: brattice; covered wooden gallery attached to the top of the external wall of a castle for defence of the base of the wall. It was supported on wooden brackets, the horizontal holes for which can sometimes be seen.

Keep   Great tower; donjon

Loop   Narrow opening to discharge arrows through or to admit light; *cross loop*, loop in the form of a cross

Merlon   Section of parapet wall between the open section of battlement, sometimes pierced with slits

Motte   Castle mound of earth or turf

Mural gallery   Gallery constructed within the thickness of a wall

Nave   Part of a church extending westwards from the screen or crossing, separated from the side aisles by pillars

Newel   Centre post or column around which winds a spiral staircase

Nook shaft   Shaft set in the angle of a pier, wall or jamb of a doorway or window

Order   Name applied to the system of base, column, capital and entablature, based on antique Greek or Roman models. There are four principal models whose details tend to follow a fixed pattern; Doric, Ionic, Composite, Corinthian

Palisade   Pailings of strong timber

Parapet   Screen or rampart covering troops from enemy observation and fire

Pilaster   Square column attached to a wall

Plinth   Projecting masonry, often with decorative mouldings, at the base of a wall

Pipe roll   Annual roll of accounts rendered at the Exchequer by sheriffs and other royal bailiffs

Portcullis   Iron-shod wooden grille suspended by chains in grooves in front of a gate and let down to ground level for additional security

Postern   Back or secondary door or gate

Quoins   Dressed stones used to finish external corners of buildings

Rebate   Recess in a door jamb into which the door fits

Relieving arch   Plain arch built into a wall above a true arch or lintel to relieve it of some of the load and thrust

Rere-wall   A protective parapet at the rear of curtain wall

Revetment   Retaining wall

Scallop   Shape in a series of curves or scallops

Sedilia   Stone seat for officiating clergy

See   Area of authority of bishop or archbishop

Siege engine   Siege machine; stone-throwing device

Springer   Lowest stone of an arch or vaulting rib

String course   Moulding or projecting band running horizontally across a façade of a building

Undercroft   Vaulted room or cellar, usually at or just below ground level

Vault   Arched ceiling or roof of stone or brick

Vice   Circular stairway; newel stairs; spiral staircase winding around a central pillar or newel post

Wainscot   Wood (normally oak) panelling on lower part of wall of a room